I0517939

ISBN 13: 978-1-955338-21-9

Cover design and illustrations
by Ava-Grace Carll

Printed in the United States of America

POCAHONTAS PRESS

CHECK, VA
WWW.POCAHONTASPRESS.COM

Feeling Amused:

Discovering the
Poetic Imagination

by

russell gregory

To my four muses:
The Divine who blessed me with
imagination,
the English teacher who nurtured me,
life with the big "L,"
and
the one

\- R.G.

Foreword

What is poetry? I don't know but I believe what is in this book gets close. That's my definition or my attempt at defining that slippery animal. Read them and if any excites your imagination, points to another way of thinking, brings tears to your eyes, elicits a yes or a no (!), sends you soaring, moves you to drop the book and walk outside full of the wonder of living, one or more may be poetry.

However, if I seem to be offering my perspective as a lecture, then that's a lecture. My friend and colleague, Rita Riddle, a poet of merit, told me I tend to end my unrevised poems with an explanation (a poem should not explain, she told me, it should inspire, elevate, excite, speak to the heart). She told me to read my poems and when I came to the sentence or sentence fragment where I started to lay out what the reader should take away (be pedantic), get rid of that, just erase that! A poet doesn't want the airplane just to taxi; a poet wants to take off and invite others along.

A word about asterisks-indicators! That's one word. Here's my explanation about their use in my table of contents and the title of the poems. One asterisk means the poem treats death and/or dying. Two asterisks belong to the poems inspired by Latin phrases (that should be obvious since the titles are Latin phrases). Three asterisks indicate a poem about love-gaining, maintaining, or losing love. Four asterisks (three are included in this collection) reveal that the structure of the poem is acrostic. No asterisks are for you to asterisk (yes, asterisk is not only a noun but a verb).

Do you want an assignment? Write some koans, short explosions of words, or a poem as an expression of your emotions during and following an event. Write until you either cry/tear up or until you almost burst with joy or anything in between. Read one of my poems and respond poetically. If you find yourself explaining what I meant or what you think-- stop, drop your pen, for you are not on a roll! Go again. However, to interpret, which brings the poem into your life and experience, that illustrates the effect on you (or, I guess, lack of effect), that speaks not only in categories of thought but also dimensions of the emotions, is to be applauded. Gusto is the stuff, for me, of the poetic art. One of the poems that always stirs me is Dylan Thomas's poem that begins: "Do not go gentle into that good night, rage, rage against the dying of the light." To know the background of the cry reflected here and to join this to his incomplete "Elegy," always and forever brings me to tears. At the same time, I long to write a poem that begins: "Do go gentle into that good night, ..."

I still need to work on that, but that's okay for I'm seeking to meld together my experience of witnessing death, of performing funerals, and the feelings that Dylan Thomas stirred within me. What suffering it was that caused him to write so personally and universally (the helplessness of his father and himself in the face of death, like the tide surging away from the shore into the depths)! Poetry is sometimes our whisper and sometimes our shout when it awakens our common humanity. Are you awake? What are your thoughts; what are your feelings that beckon to be expressed? Take a pencil and a sheet of paper and begin. Now and often.

Contents

Feeling Amused:

Discovering the
Poetic Imagination

by

russell gregory

A Friendly Acrostic for Dianna

In the midst of

My journey I stopped to
Eat at a Cracker Barrel in Jackson,
Tennessee.

Did I expect anything beyond a country meal and did
I know that the person who took my order
And delivered it to my table would seem like a
Near friend, at least so amazingly friendly that
Now, I thought, I plan to stop here (again) the next
      time I'm
At this location?

Certainly I am aware that she may treat all
      customers, not
Only me, cordially, but I did not see her
Make the same connection with another as she did
      with
Me. I am careful not to exaggerate what this meant
      and means,
As I'm a cautious guy. However,

What this encounter did to me, how it inspired me to
      visit there,
On the way back, and arrive approximately at the
      same time
When I stopped by on the way to the West,

And when seated,
Not asking beforehand to be placed in her area, I
Did scan the room repeatedly

When what to my wondering eyes did appear, but the
One and only Dianna.
Wonderful!

A Trinitarian Expression

For all you trinitarians
I've got new expressions
That makes explicit
What you believe
About the trinity:
God, Godself, Godstuff.

Ab initio (from the beginning)

I laugh for good reason;
To start from the beginning
Proves impossible for the water
Has already flowed under
The bridge and gone miles away.
And, to start from the beginning (again)
With what you have already experienced
Surely would infect that beginning.
You were not around
At the Great Beginning (Bang!),
That would be the only time
To really start from the beginning.
At our vantage point, as
Epics tell us, we were born
In Medias Res, in the middle
Of what was going on so
You have no idea how all this
Began, all the history,
All the consequences
Thereunto appertained.
You are reading here, now,
Just past the middle of this poem,
So even now the first line
Of this poem is in the past.
Life on this planet came from
A once and only beginning.
Even that was, yes,
In the middle of a time when
Much had already been decided.

Even that original beginning,
Came from some time before.
The harsh truth for those
Interested in beginnings,
There is no beginning.

Actiones secundum fidei—
action follows belief
Agere sequitur (esse)—
action follows being

Lights
Camera
Action
What is the script?
Inspired by my belief
Or arising from my experience?
Or is it written by my being,
What is fundamentally me?
Caught in the nature
Versus nurture loop?
Then the cue, give me the cue!
Lights are blazing and hot
Camera is pointed and focused
Action?
There is none.
Frozen in the knowledge
That who I am changes
With my changing beliefs and my
Experiences which shape
Who I am as I change.
Am I the chicken or the egg?
Lights
Camera
Action
Improvise.

Amygdala on fire

Amygdala on fire
Now helpless with anxiety.
The flame burning
All other emotions
And thoughts.
Burnt to a crisp.
The firemen in front
Freeze and forget their duties
Momentarily as the fire rages.
Damage control
Take charge of the breath
In deeply, out slowly
Until a deep and final
Whoosh
Blows out the blaze.
Calm at last.
You standing there
As witness
Mouth agape
How are you?

An Acrostic for lapses

Ordinarily, I'm

Sure to do the right thing
However lapses slip in at the most
Inconvenient times, and I know you are saying
Tell me about it

I am, I'm trying to ask

For forgiveness along with passing the agency
Over to you so you can decide if you are
Going to forgive me
Or cut me off because you have allowed me
Too many lapses

And I cannot deny that
Go ahead and decide then I can
Adjust either to the comfort of forgiveness or
Instead to the distress of
No grace sufficient for me

Aqua vitae (water of life)

Ponce De Leon certainly believed,
There was a spring, a flowing spring
That effervesced life back into an aging body,
And stake a claim on immortality.
Did he remember a priest
Teaching about Jesus at Jacob's well
Where he spoke of living water
To a Samaritan woman who misunderstood
As did Ponce De Leon.
Water is a necessity for living,
But not living for eternity,
Not regaining youth long gone..
If he had known the epic of Gilgamesh
He would have searched for the plant
That would have granted him
Youth in his old age, but not immortality
His quest for such a fountain,
A wily serpentine hope,
Compelled him to continue
Searching, searching, searching
As he marched toward death.

Are You?

Are you a placemarker
    or are you the chapter in a book?
        Are you the whole book
           in a library?
    Are you a library
        full of knowledge and romance,
        fiction and nonfiction,
        history and fantasy,
        self help and adventure?
Are you the author of your life,
    an account that has not yet ended,
        not yet.

    The End

At That Time

When that time comes
And you are lying in the bed,
Your breathing labored,
Your strength ebbing out,
Know that I will be standing by your side
Though you may not know that
Is not for me to say.
Know that I will be there.
But, in the case that I am the one
With failing health and near death,
Will you stand by my side?
Whether I know or do not know,
Is not for me to say,
My request and your assurance
Is quite enough

Autumn--two poems

Ah, Autumn
When the elders
Let go of certainty,
Fall to earth, and
Play like children
Rolling and tumbling,
Running and leaping
In the brisk breeze
Until they are swept
Away by the wind
To find a resting place.

On my walk,
I saw a bodhisattva
Balled up as he squatted,
Head downcast,
Looking at the grass
Reaching for a golden leaf.
As I passed by he looked
Up at me, disguised as a child,
Just able to walk,
Young enough to be pure,
Awake, and present.

Circus World

She said she viewed a cat on a stair rail.
    Doesn't she know that the world is a circus?
        That cat is not just a cat;
    that cat is the world famous Sassafras,
        the high wire aerialist.
She thinks that squirrel in that tree
    is just a squirrel.
        Pity.
He is the premier
    trapeze artist in this neighborhood.
        He doubles as a daredevil.
            Watch him as he dodges cars
            and teases dogs.
Always remember and don't forget,
    the world is a circus;
        you are always under the big top.

Dearly Departed

We stand.
We stand looking down.
We stand looking down at the dearly departed.
We say: "Little did he know he had just three more
    years."
We say: "You know the last time I saw her she was a
    picture of health."
We say: "His last words to me just before his last
    breath was 'I'm awesome.'"
We say: "I wish I had gone with her that day."
We say: "I never forgave him for what he did," or "He
    never forgave me."
We say: "She always knew just what to say."
We say: "He thought that like his mother he would
    live to one hundred."
We say: "I will miss her; she was unique,
    irreplaceable."
We say: "How will I go on without him."
We say: "How will I go on without her."
We stand looking down at the dearly departed.
We stand looking down
We stand
We offer our last words.

Death in the Wings

Again death slips into one of the wings of the stage,
    Slides across the backdrop,
    Moves into the ongoing action.
The actors proceed through their lines
    while this silent, intrusive presence stares.
Death's mouth opens;
    the characters anticipate a line
        coordinated with the scene.
        "You."
    Silence and absence, a sudden gasp
      That someone essential is missing,
        someone with the next line.
The lines scrambled.
    The cues confusing.
      The script irrelevant.
        The actors disjointed
          spitting out uncoordinated lines
   As death exits stage left momentarily.
They pause in the resounding silence
    to consider one word.
      "You."

D eath...

...d E ath

de A th...

...dea T h

deat H ...

Death is Just A Word

When that day arrives,
I will not have passed,
passed away,
passed on,
caught a pass,
I will have died.
Death is not a
curse word
or a bad word
or a toxic word,
or a scary word,
or a word to be whispered.
Death is death
pure and simple,
a part of our time,
the backend of our time.
We experience existence,
so should we not experience
non-existence,
at least of the body?
(if we agree with the people
who talk about our soul,
not the soul in Greek thought,
where soul and body are separate,
and mostly not equal,
but soul as consciousness,
something may remain)
But don't worry about all that;
concentrate on a good life so
your death will be a good death.

Dodging Responsibility

Always preparing,
though I don't know why
or what I am preparing for.
For whatever comes up?
So much happens by accident
(if you dispense with synchronicity)
suddenly or slowly building
from some event which seems
so important or pivotal
at the moment, but the effect
may be important or trivial.
What does preparation help?
Moments come one after
another and something
needs to be done, has to be done,
prepared or not one needs to act,
to respond. I was trained,
I at least knew to call emergency
services, but I walked into the hall
and saw that whale of a man
lying face down, totally still.
I was prepared for the
emergency; I was not prepared
for my response, to hide, not to help.
In that cowardly moment, I did not
want to be prepared so I could dodge
responsibility.

Entropy

In the womb, we are assembled:
We have no voice as to the design.
Pushed out without giving permission
We enter the outside world.
The next years, by starts and stops
We grow to absolute completion
And then, and then the disassembling begins.
By starts and stops the dismantling proceeds
Not noticed, for at first it may be subtle
Yet the deconstructing continues.
Now you notice hair loss or floaters
Pain in the ankle, the hip, the neck
Maybe there's blockage in the arteries
Perhaps there are digestive troubles
Loss of bladder control or worse
Nothing can stop entropy,
The slow disintegration, the inevitable.

Ex duris gloria
(from suffering [comes] glory)

Look there,
Hanging on my wall,
That framed poster
Of a mound of stones.
Atop sits a flower.
Read it.
Don't look at me;
Keep looking at the poster.
Read it.
"The obstacle is the path."
You might say: "What does it mean?"
How about "It means what it says."
"Big deal," you're nonplussed.
You are right, it is a big deal,
Actually the only deal,
Except for you it has become an obstacle,
Something to ignore,
Something to dismiss,
Something to deny.
Read it again and then again.
Read it as though you are one of the stones.
Read it as though you are the flower.
Read it as though you are water.
Read it again and then again.

Fierce Love***

Unless you've been chewed up
    and spit out,
        raked back in,
chewed up
    and spit out,
        raked back in,
            chewed up
                and spit out,
                    raked back in,
    you've not experienced
           the paroxysm
              of fierce love
                that acquaints you
                  with passion and
    silence.

Full Moon

Tonight,
    after so many months of loneliness,
        I looked up at the full moon
           for once again I was brother
      to that orb of the night.
You stood beside me,
    my sun.
          I reflected your love
            and was full.

Gestalt

People look for miracles,
    the blind to see,
    the lame to walk,
    the deaf to hear,
even the dead to arise,
    JESUS STUFF!
The real miracle is wholeness,
    when imperfect persons,
        realize they have all that they need.
        (perfection was never an attribute
            intended for humans)
        GOOD ENOUGH!
And when two imperfect persons
        love through their faults and strengths,
    they find that the whole(ness)
        is greater than the sum of the parts.

Give Me A Dog She Said

I'm a woman, a woman.
   do you hear?
I hate working with women.
     Give me a barky dog anyday.
       Tell me the plan,
       Assign me a man,
       And we'll get it done!
I don't want a pussy-cat-of-a-woman,
    However cute the term sounds,
      When we get together,
    There will be flesh and calico all over the floor.

HAIKU (as a form)—Haikus (in number)

5   Books on the three shelves
7   All the pages should be blank
5   Words get in the way

Alas, they call me a scholar; they do not know behind my words I am naked.

5   The waterfall falls
7   Still water evaporates
5   The master now drinks

The master always does the mundane for universal purposes.

5   Stalactites grow down
7   Stalagmites grow to meet them
5   The monk bumps his head

Is the monk looking down or up? He also stumps his toe.

5   One Two Three Four Five
7   One Two Three Four Five Six Seven
5   One Two Three Four Five

Some, the legalists, stick to structure without content and they are content with life diminished. They focus on the bones and forget the body.

What is more truth-full than nature; what is more beautiful than a panoramic view, particularly for me as I write in fall near the Blue Ridge Mountains?

He Sits and Listens

He sits in his chair.
He listens to that special song over and over.
He sings along.
He makes the words, his words,
Though they are not his words.
He argues.
"If they are not my words,
    they still awaken
    profound emotions
    from deepest slumber."
"But they are not my words,"
    he admits and falls silent.
He plays the song again.
He plays the song again.
And he plays the song again.

Heartthrob

I often think about how I respect you
    and honor you
        and place you on a pedestal
            but then you are out of reach.
Tonight I can only think of your twisting,
    and turning,
    and moaning,
    and groaning,
    and eyeing me,
while you smirk
when I explode inside you
and you pulsate around me,
    pulling me deeper into your heart,
    pushing me farther into mine.

How Many Times

How many times can I get it wrong?
I believe there are times when I get right.
How many times must I begin again
When I get it wrong?
What about the times I get it right?
I fix in my mind why I got it right.
At those times I say: "Now I have it!
I will never again feel sad or depressed
Or start the cascade of voices that
Dog me and harp almost endlessly
About what I did wrong AGAIN!
For whatever reason, and this
Is a mystery, sometimes hidden
In plain sight, and sometimes
Completely planted deeply in my past,
I make the wrong decision and
Act against the lessons learned.
If, like a prisoner who marks the
Days of his imprisonment
On the walls of his cell, I did the same
For all the times I got it wrong,
I would have filled every room
That I have ever entered
And still be marking now.

Howell-ing (a tribute to Diann Harris Howell)

A tornado swept into the classroom,
howling,
almost harassing (accent on the first syllable, please),
we students, nearly dying
from the roar
of nouns, pronouns, verbs,
and other parts of speech.
yet this twister didn't leave us in disarray;
this cyclone put us right
so we could write and speak our language
ordered and pristine,
not that many people cared (or care now).
we did, had to at first,
wanted to at last.
none of those in that room,
though years have passed,
can forget, shake off, disregard
that howell!

[Awakened with this little exercise, i.e.,
to take the name of my seventh grade English
teacher and work with "sound-alikes"
to craft a tribute.]

Howling = Howell (clear as the poem ends)
Harassing = Harris (reason for the accent direction)
Dying = Diann

54

I am wondering about IT

I am sitting with Alice in Wonderland
Listening to the tortoise,
The one who tortoise,
Who tortoise about IT,
About how IT is not always that IT
But this IT
Or another IT
Whatever IT is,
Whatever you identify as IT,
For IT can stand in for any thing
And IT also pulls you into a labyrinth
Filled with an infinite number of ITS.
That's the nature of IT,
Whatever IT is.
IT always exists!
That's the truth about IT.
So I'm sitting with Alice
Considering what the tortoise tortoise
About IT.

I Am Not In Love With You

I am not in love with you.
I do love your smile.
I love your laughter.
I love the way you look down at your hands as you
     talk.
I love how you point with your fingers.
I love the resolution in your steps.
I love when you blush
I maintain, though, that I am not in love with you.
I love your voice.
I love your waist [turning the dictum
     "waste not, want not," around to "waist, want").
I love your composure.
I love your thoughtfulness.
I love your caution.
I love your surprising and sudden impulsiveness.
Indeed, I love your swing between impulse and
     caution [an emotional bi-polar trait].
I love your pauses.
I love your perspicacity [I looked up the word
     to be sure I was truthful].
I love your silences.
I really, really, really love your kisses.
Let me be clear: I am not in love with you.
I love you.

I Just Don't

I don't buy cards for special occasions.
    I imagine I don't "care enough to send the very
      best."
        Cards make liars of us all.
If I receive a card,
    I don't read the printed words.
        I read what is written.
    Even some or all of that is suspect.

I Live Too Much In Solemn Prose

I live too much in solemn prose
That speaks of darkness blacker than black
That rips and tears and wounds and scars
The innocent and guilty alike,
Though all are innocent and guilty mixed.
No songs sung here, all dances nixed
No poems set free on wings of fire and ice
Harsh words with stiff punctuation
Find the curses among the blessings
Notes the pain inside the joy
Discovers rot within the holy
Though sometimes a flower grows
Between the gossamery cracks.

I read that depression is

I read that depression is
Anger turned inward.
My father worked in personnel,
A task he did well,
Yet that was far
Afield from the vocation
That had called to him
In his youth.
He loved biology and
Longed to be a physician.
He never said so;
He never told me that outright
[My mother whispered it]
Yet that yearning was there in his
Depression. Angry that
He had to provide for
His family in a job
That diminished him.
Not angry at us, his family,
Angry at fate, at circumstance
At necessity and
All the while longing
For a vocation that
Stirred the best impulses
In him. There were
Times when his depression
Took over his life,
Inspired by the distance

Between what was and
What could have been,
A tension he carried alone
So that in my inheritance,
That struggle was missing.

I Travel East

I travel East
Into the sun
Enveloped by light,
Sometimes running
For joy,
Sometimes running
From sorrow,
Quickening my pace,
Hungry for what lies ahead,
Fearful of what lurks behind,
I rush farther and farther
Into the East
Until I discover
I have arrived in the West.

I'm Tired Of Finite Time

I think of myself as infinite, yet
My age reminds me that I am in finite time.

To that end
I pledge to live each moment
Radically attentive to whatever is
Everywhere around me. If I
Do this, I'll be as close to infinite as I can be.

Immortality Assured

Zeno, the ancient philosopher,
If I can remember his paradox,
Claimed that you could never
Get to the other side of a room.
First you had to go half way.
Then you had to go half of that
And half of that, and half of that,
I believe you get the drift.
To get to the day on which I die
I have to get halfway there,
Then I have to go half of that
And half of that, there's that drift.
I will never get to the end!
I am going to be immortal!
I am immortal!
I'm never going to die!
I WILL NEVER EVER GET TO THE END!
Except I don't know the endpoint
I'm doing all my halfways toward.

In Another's Shoes (October 15, 2023)

How short my arms when I can do no more
As my love lies dying.
Her wish is no more treatment.
If that's your wish, yes, I say, yes.
And how I much love you, you know.
I love you so much more when I say Yes
For my heart says No
But not to you, to your cancer.
This blight that began in secret
And when the signs were irrefutable
I began to know what helpless meant
And hope, and defeat and victory for a while.
And now this, this place and time, now.
I ask for grace, for a peaceful death
An end to the pain, the suffering,
The days that are a lifetime long and the way to the
end of life,
The beginning of sorrow, of the absence of presence.
All I can know tonight is that my love for you
Right at this moment, forever links us,
For you won't die to me, you will always live in me.

Instructions for my sons after my death

When that day comes,
And it most assuredly will.
When I am no longer here,
Both when my death is fresh
And as it recedes into the past
As it most assuredly will
And quicker than you realize,
Find a photograph,
One that you treasure,
One of me, or you and me, or
The gathered family,
Or a large group of people
In which I am looking
At the camera, at you;
Feel free to talk to me
As often as you want or need
Unfettered by pride or shame
Or guilt or joy or delight or
Any of the myriad feelings that will
Rise in you, especially those emotions
That bind us together.
Still.

Jimmy Stewart's Line

Jimmy Stewart's love interest, Elizabeth, played by Barbara Stanwyck, gazes at his character. Every feature and movement of her face coaxes his feelings out as he shows his discomfort. In that moment he says: "You know, uh, I've been uh, thinking uh, uuuhhh, about how you and me, no, no, that's not right, and you being an English teacher, you must think I'm a dope, well, anyway, I've been going over and over in my mind about how you and I have been seeing each other for quite, uh, quite a while, and I just thought, gee, have I already said that, I just thought, there I go again, I just was sitting there, you know, no you wouldn't know because I haven't told you, I was in the front porch swing, just sitting there swaying back and forth, when it hit me, and even though I didn't run right over, I thought about it, I must do a lot of thinking, that's what my mother says and then she tells me to do something, you know, spontaneously, without dwelling on it for so long, so I was sitting in the swing, uh, I've said that, when it came to me like I had known it for only a moment, and yet for a long time, that, uh, that, that, that, that I, uh love you, yes that's exactly it, exactly what hit me, I love you Elizabeth." Barbara would smile, pull him to her and kiss him.

CUT!

[Fortunately, Jimmy Stewart was not Hamlet. Just imagine his soliloquy! The play would have taken several days!]

Life Does Not
(August 9, 2023 to Cindy Roberts Bragg)

Life does not provide a list
Of all the friends you will know
Of all the moments you will share
Of all the thoughts and feelings you will ignite
Of all the consequences of your actions
Of all the joy and all the sorrow you will live through
Of all the memories you will own
Of all those memories
Of the friends and the moments and the thoughts
      and the feelings and the consequences and
      the joy and sorrow that
You contain.
The end.
No.
Not the end if you compile a list,
A list that you begin checking off the names of the
departed, friends not forgotten and moments and
thoughts and feelings and consequences and joy and
sorrow.
      Until someone notices that you too are gone
      though some friends remain, friends who
      shared those moments and thoughts and
      feelings and consequences and joy and
      sorrow.
And something there never dies.
Never.
Something remains.
Something does remain.
Something.

Living Among Ghosts

I am living among ghosts
Father, a ghost since 1998, now embraces mother
She returned to his side six years ago,
His embrace much more tender since death brings
Time and time to bear on what was misunderstood,
Unseen, passed over, neglected.
As soon as I sense them, a whole crowd
Arrives and I recognize every one as they brush past.
Tonight as I sit, a crowd of spirits visit me.
They ask questions; they claim they need to know.
I'm not fooled; I know their questions are statements,
Obvious rhetorical questions, for their queries
Point to what I'm not seeing, not hearing,
Not understanding, not doing.
Their lips move as they form the words
"Carpe Diem" but I see "memento morii."

Lucky Charms

Funny what our lucky charms are;
    funny when we think our lives run on luck.
How many years ago
    did I exit the wrong door on the first day of school,
        see the wrong metal policeman
            escorting me across the street,
                and walk in a direction
            perpendicular
                    to the way home?

I picked up a spent matchbook,
    and deemed it my lucky charm to guide me
            home.
I wandered on
    as I grew more fearful and realized I was lost.
        An acquaintance from that first day, when he
           saw me,
           rescued me
                and took me to his home.
His mother called mine to assure her I was safe.
I didn't save that matchbook.
    You'd think I would have.
        It's long gone.
I possess a memory that surfaces from time to time,
    the recollection of a boy lost and found,
        and a reminiscence that reminds me
            of the grace of friendship
                which redeems when luck runs out.

Lucky Penny

I'm crazy to say I hurt my dad only once.
    For every wound I received,
        he carried one from his childhood.
            Many of his wounds were complications
                of guilt as he plied his task as
                    parent.
We're all the blind leading the blind,
    or the wounded limping alongside the wounded.
But I stabbed him in his heart,
        when I stood before his "good deeds"
        calendar
           in our kitchen
and laughed at his task for the day.
        He was to take twenty pennies and
                toss them on the ground
           as he went through his schedule
                so that someone would find a
                "lucky penny"
                    and feel refreshed
I said that I would never pick up another penny.
        "Planted pennies are not lucky pennies!"
    My father winced.
Just the other day I squatted down next to a child
who had seen
    a copper coin on the ground.
        We both had our knees up,
           our bottoms inches from the ground.
        We both looked in wonder,
           the child's genuine, mine reflected.

The child looked from the coin to me and back again,
    each time her smile growing more wondrously
magical.

"A penny," she blurted out, as though she had
            found
        the Hope Diamond in her sandpile.
"A lucky penny," I added.
She snatched it up, stood straight up,
        shoved it in the pocket of her smock.
She screeched and clapped her hands as she sang:
    "A lucky penny, a lucky penny, a lucky
        penny."
I watched her run to tell everyone about her stroke of
        luck.
    I whispered: "Thank you, Dad."

Meretrix
[Prostitute or one who earns]

Meretrix, the Latin term for prostitute
Sounds like "merry tricks,"
That's what they aim to do.
The literal meaning is "one who earns,"
But from sexual prowess.
In our culture, this meaning
Takes on a negative sense,
One who earns the disdain,
The negative judgment, the
Heaped scorn that can lead to violence.
A book on my shelf claims
Prostitution is like any other
Profession a woman may choose
Except she earns more and
Maintains control over her
Business and her Body,
Except those enslaved by a pimp.
Some would indeed paint sex work
As sordid, drug infested, tightly
Controlled by pimps with the women
Or men (did you think a whore
Was just women?) ensnared.
There is that surely,
However, that's a picture
Plagued by inaccuracy and stereotype.
Many prostitutes would say
Their "work" is about joy,
The appreciation of sexuality unfettered.

Many take the place of a therapist,
Some become cult prostitutes,
The incarnation of the Goddess.

Missing Her
(For a grieving friend)

Just take a moment to
Understand how our lives play out quickly.
Do you find that you sometimes try to
        slow time or stop
It so you can remain in a tender moment for
The rest of your life and only celebrate that
        one precious moment?
However, you may remember there were many
        moments like that

And you bargained for one forever moment
        not several.
Now that would force you to reconsider
        your decision to
Not honor all those other magic moments,
        to just ignore them

By and by
You might begin to realize that the ups and downs
In life color each other, the ups challenge the downs,
I'm not
Naïve, and the downs bring the ups into focus,
        showing how
Good and precious
They are. So in living and in our memories
Our task is to treasure our complete life, all of it,
Now, until that last breath.

Moments of Certitude

A moment of certitude
Crept up behind me,
Grabbed me by the shoulder
And spun me around
So I was face to face
With the mirror of myself.
        Aha
        Eureka
        Oh
        Oh
        Oh shit!
All along, all along that was it?
    THAT?
    IT!
I was blind, not looking
In that direction
That direction!
        Aha
        Eureka
        Oh
        Oh
        Oh
        Ooooh.

Mortuis non dolere (the dead do not grieve)

He is still; she lies silent
No breath there
The chest neither rises nor falls
The body unmoving
Eyes closed, lips taut
The hands crossed
Softness replaced by stone hardness
When spoken to, no reply
What is missing from the dead?
Grief, simply grief.
The dead do not grieve;
They do not need to grieve

My Brother

My Brother is never far from me
Though in his lifetime (he has died)
We were never close.
A wall of the unsaid between us,
With portraits of misunderstanding
And distrust hung on that wall.
I stood before the mirror in the bathroom
And looked down at my left hand
Fingers, not as thick as his,
Formed a pose that transformed me
Into my brother who was a man
Who worked with his hands.
My brother is never far from me.

My Father Greets Me

My father, when eating breakfast
   and the obligations of the coming day
   settled on him,
      would bend his head forward,
      place three fingers on his forehead,
         his thumb on his cheek
         while the little finger was left to roam,
            the one part of his hand out of the box,
            and ponder.

Perhaps he pondered, I don't know,
   I merely observed.
         If he sensed my presence
         or heard my footsteps,
         his head would whip around,
         his hand remained
         suspended in its place
         as though he had two heads—
         the one that remained in place
         and the one that greeted me with
         a warm smile and an enthusiastic
         "Good morning son."

I merely observed until today,
   when eating breakfast
      my father greeted me in his gesture
         as I leaned on my hand and pondered.

Fas est et ab hoste doceri
(it is lawful to be taught,
even by an enemy)

If, as the Zen Buddhists say,
the obstacle is the path,
then one's enemy (enemies) is (are)
precisely the best teacher(s).
I do not mean to say that I should learn
how to be crass and cruel
to be hateful, malevolent, murderous,
and unrepentantly evil,
but to learn what lies within myself,
resides in my frustration and anger.
My sense of being cheated, maligned,
taken advantage of, or tossed aside
might build within me and take its strength from un-
controlled malefic humours.
The shadow side, undisclosed and
festering, exercising its power
by acts of mischief and displays
of violence, even to its own kind.
Once disclosed and drained of its animosity, becomes
a force for altruism.
Test this by surveying the wise
near and far.
Was it not Lincoln who said that
to rid yourself of enemies, you should
make them your friends?
Was it not Gandhi who said to befriend
your enemy is true religion?

Was it not Oscar Wilde who said
to forgive your enemies for it annoyed them, his un-
derhanded recommendation?
Was it not Jesus who said
to love your enemies?
Was it Zen Buddhism that said
the true enemy is within?
So that inner enemy is the true threat
every waking hour.
Was it Frost who said that there are
two roads that lead into the forest?
The wide one, the one usually traveled,
banal by its overuse making the
surroundings invisible.
The narrow one, the road not usually taken,
difficult, uninviting, perhaps overgrown,
filled with shadows, dark and foreboding,
not seemingly a friend to the traveler, but
oh so illuminating.

No Sting

The smiling man,
    sitting across the room,
        the one with no hair,
            claims he has befriended death.
How is that done?
    "How" is difficult to explain.
He added that Lincoln did explain it
        but he readily admitted he was not Lincoln.
"The way you rid yourself of enemies is to make them
your friends,"
    or something like that he exclaimed.
                The explanation?
                The explanation!
Death was never an enemy to Lincoln,
        but a natural complement to life,
            an intimate friend, like in Genesis,
           a helpmate.
Always near,
Always present,
Always a necessity,
Always an accompaniment to the dance of living.
That's why death had no sting for him.
That why he still lives.
No sting,

Non Sic Dormit, Sed Vigilat
[Sleeps not but is awake]

Having sadly left behind the fiction of youth,
    faux immortality,
I count every grain of sand that drops through the
    narrow neck of my hourglass.
I use a timer on my watch that segments time into
    separate units
        and the seconds tick down to zero
            only to reset.
I make a list in the morning of tasks that
    I yearn to accomplish.
I know the days ahead are few
    compared to those behind.
I sometimes work in a daze considering what was
    done and what was not.
I live feverishly with the sword of Damocles dangling,
    swinging, overhead.
I divine the inviolable in mortality,
    as the sand runs out.

Not The Same

Someone happy this way came
    and when she left i was not the same.
       person i was when she went through
    happens to know she was not the same too.

[If "she" is not capitalized except at the beginning of
a sentence, then why should "i" which stands for me,
be capitalized except at the beginning of a sentence?]

Nulla Dies Sine Linea
(Not a day without a line drawn)

Who said that temptation, once
shunned, departs forever.
My experience differs and experience
holds the final judgment.
Each day brings challenges
fashioned for that day in dazzling
colors for the eyes, pungent
fragrance for the nose and
ambrosial flavors for taste.
These three lure one to embrace all,
luxuriate beyond reason.
The colors, if witnessed with sober,
critical observation, soon blind.
The fragrance soon overwhelms and
dulls to the point of anosmia.
Soon the tongue forgets
the distinctions sweet, salty, sour, bitter.
Temptation does just that, blinds,
dulls, and embitters sooner or later.
In Eden, the prudent woman drew a line
so as not to yield to temptation.
Not to touch meant not to eat and
thus honor the prohibition
Yet she erased the line when
convinced she, they, could be gods.
Would that she had drawn a thicker line.

PRO...
CRAS...
TIN...
ATI

Omne Initum Difficile Est
[Every Beginning Is Difficult]

Who has said this-
"Every beginning is difficult"?
Almost everyone.
Everyone?
Not true,
But some have anyway.
Am I making a mountain
Out of a molehill?
Not exactly.
Mountain is mountain,
Mole hill is mole hill.
Either takes requisite labor,
Either requires the first step
For other steps to follow.
Task takes risk,
Kierkegaard's leap!
The hero's quest,
Even in the most menial.

Omnia Aponte Fluant,
Absit violentia Rebus
[Everything Should Flow By Itself,
Force Should Be Absent]

Relentless focus on control
When the yard is compromised by weeds.
Compromised? Weeds?
A purchase of carcinogenic spray
Gives me the power to eradicate
And transform my lawn.
I become, in the process,
Executioner of countless worms
That feed a thousand robins
And so on and so on up the chain
Until I have wounded
Nature I sought to perfect
In my own way.
The remaining poison stored
Until the time I discover
How to dispose of it safely,
If that is possible.
Time passes and the worms
Return slowly, then the robins,
And so on and so on up the chain.
The lawn heals and keeps
Me under surveillance.

Only a shadow

I am only a shadow on the wall
in the sunlight that enters my study
through the window behind me.
The chair I sit in, a shadow.
If I were to sit here all day
as the light shifted to the west,
my shadow would slide across the wall.
When the sun dipped over
the horizon and night emerged,
My shadow would merge with
the darkness and disappear,
absorbed in the longest shadow of all.

Our Lives In Two Moments

Slow motion (imagine it)—
    the head drops down
    then sweeps up to the left
    the eyes close in the first half of a blink
    the mouth begins to form the word "hello"
    the eyes begin to open
     you have vanished.
I am in slow motion in a fast motion landscape.
     Again.
I roll to a stop at a stoplight.
I feel the car rock forward
    then back as I turn my head to the left.
A random woman in a car,
    a complete stranger,
    turns her head to the right.
Our eyes meet
    and for a moment our lives join.
        We court
        We fall in love
        We marry
        We have children
        We raise them to be passionate
        We send them off to enter their own lives
We glance back at the light,
    a synchronic movement,
        it is green.
    I turn back and you are gone.
I am in slow motion in a fast motion landscape.

Per Volar Sonata
[Born To Soar]

Witness Icarus, jubilant with the thrill of flight,
Soaring into the heavens to kiss the sun,
Noticing the hot wax running down his arms,
Feeling the feathers loosen
Realizing the folly of his arrogance
Remembering his father's cautionary words
Flailing and falling faster as his wings disintegrate
Longing for help that will not come
Hearing his father's voice cry out
Sensing the sea rising up to meet him
Glancing toward land he'll never reach
Spying a figure pushing a boulder up a hill
Crashing finally into the restless sea
Saying to himself as he sinks:
"I wish I were he."
As feathers float on the waves.

Quid quid recipitur ad modum
recipientis reciptur
(What is received, is received in the
manner of the receiver)

Philosophers call it epistemology
How we know and what we know.
Being taught what to know however
Tells us nothing about what's actually there,
What's out there or over there or in there.
Your instructor didn't get the *ding an sich*
From their teachers who taught them
So you're not going to get it either
And that is not factoring in
What the teachers received was
Colored or affected by their ability
To receive and the same goes for me,
Not to speak of the teachers before
And after me.
Turtles all the way up and down.
One time and one time only,
When we are closest to
Capturing the *ding an sich.*
Is as a very young child who
Knows no names, who just experiences *THAT*,
One with the world, inseparable.

Schrödinger's cat

Both you and I are Schrodinger's cat;
We are in a box called living.
So like Schrodinger's cat we may be
Dead or alive and probably both dead and alive.
I'm thinking of Samuel whom I believed to be alive,
But Samuel is dead and has been for quite some time
I imagined that Suzanne was dead, most likely
For I remember how she burned her candle
       at both ends.
However, Suzanne is alive and in very good health.
I am glad Suzanne is very much alive.
[I lament Samuel's death].
Suzanne may imagine me dead,
And she not the only one.
Yet I am most assuredly not dead,
That is, no obituary has been printed.
Many know I am still alive and breathing,
though others just don't know.
I'm practically dead to them, at least gone
Forever from their lives.
One with Schrodinger's cat,
Dead or alive, dead and alive.

[According to quantum mechanics, a subatomic
particle like an electron can be anywhere and
everywhere at once, and a cat can be both alive and
dead in a box until it is observed.--FR. NYT]

Scio me nihil scire—I know that I know nothing

A distinguished professor once said:
"Graduates who have just received their Ph.D.
should never write a major work until they
have taught at least ten years.
He continued: "I published too soon in
my career. When I read much
of what I wrote I didn't know who
wrote that book, that article,
that piece, but he was ill-informed,
or thick as a brick. As I have
lived and considered the power
of thoughts, of feelings, of words,
I discovered I know less and less."
Look at Al Ghazali, the greatest
authority in Islam at his time,
who left his teaching post for
the thrill of ecstasy and knowing
all that he knew was nothing, a barrier
to true knowledge. If you don't
trust Islam, how about Acquinas who
toward the end of a distinguished
life of theological observations,
treatises that shaped the Catholic
Church, claimed that all his knowledge
was worthless, wrong, superfluous
to the true knowledge of God.
This is agnosticism, the fruit of old age,
so sweet, so very sweet.

Since We Returned To Our Sensuous

Infatuation carries
   a cartload of sensuosity.
If that doesn't ring true for you,
     get infatuated.
More to the point,
   fall in love deeply.
If you do,
   make time
     and energy your friend,
       for the intimacy of love requires
       active attention.
If you spend your time,
   being mad,
   being distracted,
   being tired,
   being busy,
   being frustrated,
     you drain the sensuousness,
       the sinnlichkeit,
       the sensual,
       the sanselig,
       the synhwyrus,
     right out of the equation
       so that $2x + xy = ZZZZZZ$.
Fortunately you and I,
   after a short holiday,
     returned to the sensuous,.
We've parked our minds,
   and embraced each other bawdily.

[The foreign words in order are German, French, Danish, and
      Welsh]

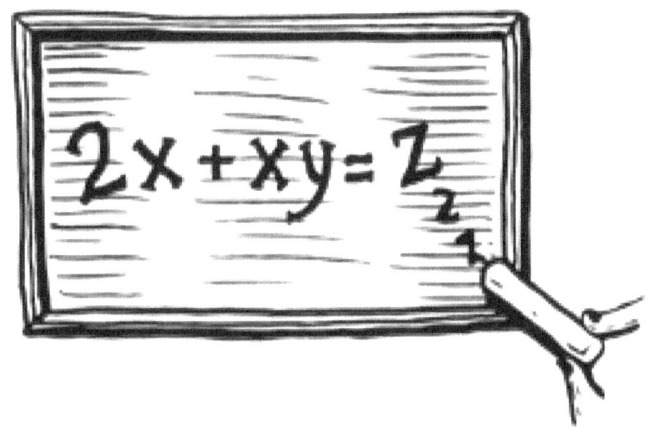

Stultilo Quium (foolish talk)

Talking crazy, making no sense,
Spinning tales, lying,
Yelling angrily,
Saying whatever comes to mind,
Finding words just to please,
Droning on and on,
Yada, yada, yada.
Describing the indescribable,
Making small talk even smaller,
Being a motor mouth,
Repeating yourself for emphasis,
Etcetera, etcetera, etcetera.
Relating what just occurred,
Or earlier in the day,
Or, yesterday or last week,
Or, that one slight from years ago,
That just won't let go,
Blah, blah, blah.
Giving little thought to grammar,
Interrupting non sequitur,
Stopping mid-sentence then
Beginning another thought,
And so on and so forth.
Have you time to waste on foolish talk
And what not?

That Cat
(for Diann Howell)

That cat,
That cat's head swings left and right
As she watches me chase a fly
Around the empty kitchen,
Whipping the flyswatter right and left,
Slapping table, wall, and cabinet,
Swatting to no avail.
The cat watches from her perch on the countertop.
Is that a Cheshire smile spreading across her face?
I retire to a chair and slump to rest
And the cat watches,
Watches me,
Watches the fly,
Head moving on an arc left and right
Suddenly, a leap
On her way to the floor the fly vanishes.
A Cheshire smile crosses my lips
As she glances at me and licks her paw.

The Feelings' Escape

An imperceptible voice signals
    the beginning of the feeling's escape.
They,
    joy, sadness, calm, panic, hatred, love,
    disdain, humility,
        rush from the prison deep inside logic
            and poised demeanor.
They rush down the corridors of control,
    until they break down the walls of inhibition
        and prohibition
    into the bright light of being true,
        of being actual,
        of being genuine,
        of being present,
        of being passionate!

The Finger and the Moon

The
Finger
That
Points
At
The
Moon
Is
Not
The
Moon.
The
Moon
That
a
finger
points
toward
does
not
depend
upon
that
finger.
The
moon

and
the
finger
are
not.
the
point,
the
master
pointed
out.
Point
Taken
replied
the
student
holding
a
flower
and
smiling.

The Past is a foreign country

The past is now a foreign country;
The language is unintelligible.
Once we spoke it fluently
For we lived there and
Called it the present or right now.
We did not know that this, our new
Present, clouded the memories and
Consigned them to the misty swamp
Of lost opportunities, faulty choices,
And, yes, moments of bliss.
I'll grant you those delights but
Sometimes those remembered moments
Were drained of vitality bit by bit.
Terrain that once was known
Through the senses, now
Trips us up again and again.
We find ourselves crawling
After each fall backwards. Watch out!
That place once multi-colored
And replete with riches
Has become so barren,
Filled with depressions so deep
They trap you. Losing direction,
You can get lost and never return,
Or, return, changed and mournful
Some insist they can
Travel to that distant place,
The past, even further
To their origin and they remember

The language, can walk the
        treasured landscape, or even run,
And when sated with the memories
Return refreshed and thankful.
Not me.

The Secret

The secret is hidden in the old mantra of Siam
Found scratched on the wall of a cave.
Impossible to understand for the
        language was unknown.
A specialist in ancient languages,
        Dr. Samuel Schönerfurz,
The one who discovered Rosetta Stone II,
Volunteered to decipher the inscription.
The rock wall had an account recorded
        in three languages:
Perpetua; Gujarati Sangam, and Wingding.
Gujarati Sangam ranks as the
        second oldest language,
Wingding the most ancient.
Fortunately, Perpetua, the most recent,
        which derives from Pig Latin, and
Gajurati Sangam from Sandschrift, are widely
        known from former studies.
Still, one letter remains to be identified from
The mantra, one not included in the other accounts,
Apparently from some ritual peculiar to the
Siamese who wrote in Wingding.

[The mantra, still incomplete, remains a mystery.
At this time, based on Rosetta Stone II,
we have this:

    "O W__H T__ GOO SIAM"

(For your information, you who have inquiring minds, Doctor S. also assisted in the translation of the inscription on the pedestal which described the down fall of Ozymandias Jr.]

To Sit With A Son

"Do you want to sit (meditate)
just for ten minutes," my son asked.
"Maybe in the morning when
we are fresh," I replied.
"Just ten minutes, it would mean
so much to me to sit now."
"Of course. Let's sit."
He went and got a chair so
that we could follow the
Plum Village way.
I focused on a rock, my favorite rock,
my pet rock that is affected by
anicca, anatta, and dukkha just like us.
He closed his eyes and began to float,
his red hair porcupining upward
and outward, threading all
that exists together.
Soon, he touched my thigh.
I glanced at my watch,
eight minutes and some.
"Maybe we didn't make it to ten,
but it was complete," he whispered
and hugged me.
Eight, ten, what does it matter
when you have traversed
eternity with a son.

From a letter to my Son, Andrew.

I know this is not a real poem
[or maybe it is one of your mother's
amalgamated thought poems],
but it gathered together a few of my thoughts. I
think of you often and hope that your way is chal-
lenging and rewarding.
You're such a good son [MAN] and I love you.]

Tweener

From time to time she would ask:
   "Am I a tweener?"
      The divorce behind me and dating before me,
         she wanted to know if she would be
            a stepping
                 stone
                    to
                       the
                          next
                             one
who would be a keeper.
    A few times with a quavering voice,
        she would announce,
      though the question lingered close behind,
        "I know I'm a tweener,"
                  followed by
     "but I don't care.
        I'm having a wonderful time with you."
This afternoon I found out the truth
   when she tweened me,
      suspending me between
    "I don't know what happened,"
      and
        "I don't know why."

*Van Gogh's Self-portrait with Grey Felt Hat
(dedicated to Diann Harris Howell)*

I don't own Van Gogh's
"Self-portrait with Grey Felt Hat."
However a poster advertising the
Immersive presentation of
His art in Charlotte, North Carolina
Hangs over my toilet in my downstairs
Half bathroom.
I speak with him regularly
And he stares impassively.
I wait for a reply and only silence greets me,
A greeting nonetheless.
I had always looked at his left side
(right side if you look straight on)
Yet this particular day I noticed the dark strokes
And a malformed eye on his right side
(left side if you look straight on.)
That side reflected the thoughts
Which drove him nearly mad,
Deep into depression and self-hatred.
(His logical side was his demon self)
Ecstasy shone in his other side.
For a while, all I could see was the monster.
Now, I hold the two together,
Embrace them both,
The shadow and the luminous.

We stand

We stand.
We stand looking down.
We stand looking down at the dearly departed.
We say: "Little did he know he had just three more years."
We say: "You know the last time I saw her she was a picture of health."
We say: "His last words to me just before his last breath was 'I'm awesome.'"
We say: "I wish I had gone with her that day."
We say: "I never forgave him for what he did," or "He never forgave me."
We say: "She always knew just what to say."
We say: "He thought that like his mother he would live to one hundred."
We say: "I will miss her; she was unique, irreplaceable."
We say: "How will I go on without him."
We say: "How will I go on without her."
We stand looking down at the dearly departed.
We stand and offer our last words
We stand looking down
We stand still.

Wedding Blessing

May you live in reality, not in a dream,
    but may you dream.
May you love each other singularly
        and wonderfully
             so that your love encompasses
                all who cross your path.
May you take your whole life together
    to live your lives.

I DO
I DO
I AM
I DO
I DO
I DO
I AM
I AM
I AM
I AM
I DO
I DO
I DO
I AM
I AM
I DO
I DO
I AM

When

When I say I'm not thinking of her,
    I am.
When I say I will never think of her again,
    I do.
When I fill up my mind with thoughts so I don't have
room for her,
    I do.
When I no longer want to be at her mercy,
    I am.

When I Die What Not To Say

When I die
Do not say
He has passed away
Or passed on
Or he has passed
Or he has kicked the
　　bucket
Or I am asleep
Or I look asleep
Or I've been awakened to
　　eternal life
Or God called me home
Or I went before my time
(How dare you challenge
　　God's time!)
Or I bit the dust
Or I bought the farm
　　(where there's
　　plenty of dust)
Or I bought a
　　one-way ticket
Or I breathed my last
　　(that's a major duh,
　　I mean really!)
Or gave up the ghost
Or got my wings
Or my number was up.
(Was that the same one
　　as in the draft lottery?)

Or lost my life
(does that mean I can
    find it with your help?)
Or playing a harp
Or pushing up daisies
    (I plan to have an acorn
    in my pocket for an oak)
Or took a permanent
    vacation
Or any other euphemisms
Those signal (and tries to hide)
    the angst
Of the comment's owner.
Look, I am not
somewhat dead
Or mostly dead
Or clinically dead
But really dead.
I died, folks.
That's what you can say
    or publish or disseminate.
He died.
He is dead.
He doesn't *live* here
    anymore.

www.ingramcontent.com/pod-product-compliance
Lightning Source LLC
Chambersburg PA
CBHW031529120626
46545CB00005B/2057